THE ATLANTIS: MYTHS, LEGENDS, AND HISTORY

GOLU KUMAR

Copyright © Golu Kumar
All Rights Reserved.

Contents

THE legend of Atlantis, an island continent in the Atlantic Ocean next to the Pillars of Hercules that was once the center of a powerful empire before it was submerged by the sea, has served as the inspiration for many extravagant theories and continues to pique people's interest throughout the centuries. To commemorate the successful passage of four centuries since Christopher Columbus first set foot on Western shores, the 12th of October 1892 has been declared a global holiday. The journey has been called the most memorable in the history of our race, and the century that has since come to an end is richer than any that came before it in terms of the changes that the passage of time has revealed since the union of the New and the Old Worlds. The story of the Lost Atlantis is recorded in the _Timæus_ and, with many fanciful amplifications, in the _Critias_ of Plato. According to the dialogues, as reproduced there, Critias repeats to Socrates a story told him by his grandfather, then an old man of ninety, when he was not more than ten years of age. According to this narrative, Solon visited the city of Sais, at the head of the Egyptian delta, and there learned from the priests of the ancient empire of Atlantis, and its overthrow by a convulsion of nature. "No one," says Professor Jowett, in his critical edition of _The Dialogues of Plato_, "knew better than Plato how to invent a noble lie'"; and he, unhesitatingly, pronounces the whole narrative a fabrication. "The world, like a child, has readily, and for the most part, unhesitatingly accepted the tale of the Island of Atlantis." To the critical editor, this reception furnishes only an illustration of popular credulity, showing how the chance word of a poet or philosopher may give rise to endless historical or religious speculation. In the _Critias_, the legendary tale is unquestionably expanded into details of no possible historical significance or genuine antiquity. But it is not without reason, that men like Humboldt have recognized in the original legend the possible vestige of a widely-spread tradition of earliest times. In this respect, at any rate, I purpose here to review it.

It is to be noted that even in the time of Socrates, and indeed of the elder Critias, this Atlantis was referred to as the vague and inconsistent tradition of a remote past; though not more inconsistent than much else which the cultured Greeks were accustomed to receiving. Mr. Hyde Clarke, in an "Examination of the Legend," printed in the _Transactions of the Royal Historical Society_, concludes that Atlantis was the name of the king rather than of the dominion. But king and kingdom have ever been liable to be referred to under a common designation. According to the account in the _Timæus_, Atlantis was a continent lying over against the Pillars of Hercules, greater in extent than Libya and Asia combined; the highway to other islands and to a great ocean, of which the Mediterranean Sea was a mere harbor. But in the vagueness of all geographical knowledge in the days of Socrates and Plato, this Atlantic domain is confused with some Iberian or western African power, which is stated to have been arrayed against Egypt, Hellas, and all the countries bordering on the Mediterranean Sea. The knowledge even of the western Mediterranean was then very imperfect; and, to the ancient Greek, the West was a region of vague mystery which sufficed for the localization of all his fondest imaginings. There, on the far horizon, Homer pictured the Elysian plain, where, under a serene sky, the favorites of Zeus enjoyed eternal felicity; Hesiod assigned the abode of departed heroes to the Happy Isles beyond the western waters that engirdled Europe, and Seneca foretold that that mysterious ocean would yet disclose an unknown world which it then kept concealed. To the ancients, Elysium ever lay beyond the setting sun; and the Hesperia of the Greeks, as their geographical knowledge increased, continued to recede before them into the unexplored west.

In the youth of all nations, the poet and historian are one; and, according to the tale of the elder Critias, the legend of Atlantis was derived from a poetic chronicle of Solon, whom he pronounced to have been one of the best of poets, as well as the wisest of men. The elements of oral tradition are aptly outlined in the dialogue which Plato puts into the mouth of Timæus of Locris, a Pythagorean philosopher. Solon is affirmed to have told the tale to his personal friend, Dropidas, the great-grandfather of Critias, who repeated it to his son; and he, eighty years thereafter, in extreme old age, told it to his grandson, a boy of ten, whose narrative, reproduced in mature years, we are supposed to read in the dialogue of the _Timæus_. Even those are but the later links in the traditionary catena. Solon himself visited Sais, a city of the Egyptian delta, under the protection of the goddess, Neith or Athene. There, when in converse with the Egyptian priests, he learned, for the first time, rightly to appreciate how ignorant of antiquity he and his countrymen were. "O Solon, Solon," said an aged priest to him, "you Hellenes are ever young, and there is no old man who is a Hellene; there is no opinion or tradition of knowledge among you which is white with age." Solon had told them the mythical tales of Phoroneus and Niobe, and Deucalion and Pyrrha, and had attempted to reckon the interval by generations since the great deluge. But the priest of Sais replied to this that such Hellenic annals were children's stories. Their memory went back but a little way, and recalled only the latest of the great convulsions of nature, by which revolutions in past ages had been wrought: "The memory of them is lost because there was no written voice among you." And so the venerable priest undertook to tell him of the social life and condition of the primitive Athenians 9000 years before. It is among the events of this older era that the overthrow of Atlantis is told: a story already "white with age" in the time of Socrates, 3400 years ago. The warriors of Athens, in that elder time, were a distinct caste; and when the vast power of Atlantis was marshaled against the Mediterranean nations, Athens bravely repelled the invader, and gave liberty to the nations whose safety had been imperiled; but in the convulsion that followed, in which the island-continent was engulfed in the ocean, the warrior race of Athens also perished.

The story, as it thus reaches us, is one of the vaguest of popular legends, and has been transmitted to modern times in the most obscure of all the writings of Plato. Nevertheless, there is nothing improbable in the idea that it rests on some historic basis, in which the tradition of the fall of an Iberian, or other aggressive power in the western Mediterranean, is mingled with other and equally vague traditions of intercourse with a vast continent lying beyond the Pillars of Hercules. Mr. Hyde Clarke, in his _Khita and Khita-Peruvian Epoch_, draws attention to the ancient system of geography, alluded to by various early writers, and notably mentioned by Crates of Pergamos, B.C. 160, which treated the Four Worlds. This connects with the statement by Mr. George Smith, derived from the cuneiform interpretations, that Agu, an ancient king of Babylonia, called himself "King of the Four Races." He also assigns to it a relation with others, including its Inca equivalent of _Tavintinsuzu_, the Empire of the Four Quarters of the World. But the extravagance of regal titles has been the same in widely diverse ages; so much caution is necessary before they can be made a safe basis for comprehensive generalizations. Four kings made war against five in the vale of Siddim; and when Lot was despoiled and taken captive by Chedorlaomer, King of Elam, Tidal, King of Nations, and other regal allies, Abraham, with no further aid than that of his trained servants, born in his house, three hundred and eighteen in all, smote their combined hosts, and recovered the captives and the spoil. Here, at least, it is obvious that "the King of Nations" was somewhat on a par with one of the six vassal kings who rowed King Edgar on the River Dee. Certainly, within any early period of authentic history, the conceptions of the known world were reduced within narrow bounds; and it would be a very comprehensive deduction from such slight premises as the legend supplies, to refer to an age of accurate geographical knowledge in which the western hemisphere was known as one of four worlds, or continents. When the Scottish poet, Dunbar, wrote of America, twenty years after the voyage of Columbus, he only knew of it as "the new-found isle."

The opinion, universally favored in the infancy of physical science, of the recurrence of convulsions of nature, whereby nations were revolutionized, and vast empires destroyed by fire or engulfed in the ocean, revived with the theories of cataclysmic phenomena in the earlier speculations of modern geology; and has even now its advocates among writers who have given little heed to the concurrent opinion of later scientific authorities. Among the most zealous advocates of the idea of a submerged Atlantic continent, the seat of a civilization older than that of Europe, or the old East, was the late Abbé Brasseur de Bourbourg. As an indefatigable and enthusiastic investigator, he occupies a place in the history of American archæology somewhat akin to that of his fellow countryman, M. Boucher de Perthes, about the palæontological disclosures of Europe. He had the undoubted merit of first drawing the attention of the learned world to the native transcripts of Maya records, the full value of which is only now being adequately recognized. His _Histoire des Nations Civilisées_ aims at demonstrating from their religious myths and historical traditions the existence of a self-originated civilization. In his subsequent _Quatre Lettres sur le Mexique_, the Abbé adopted, in the most literal form, the venerable legend of Atlantis, giving free rein to his imagination in some very fanciful speculations. He calls into being, "from the vasty deep," a submerged continent, or, rather, an extension of present America, stretching eastward, and including, as he deems probable the Canary Islands, and other insular survivals of the imaginary Atlantis. Such speculations of unregulated zeal are unworthy of serious consideration.

But it is not to be wondered at that the vague legend, so temptingly outlined in the _Timæus_, should have kindled the imaginations of a class of theorists, who, like the enthusiastic Abbé, are restrained by no doubts suggested by scientific indications. So far from geology lending the slightest confirmation to the idea of an engulfed Atlantis, Professor Wyville Thomson has shown, in his _Depths of the Sea_, that while oscillations of the land have considerably modified the boundaries of the Atlantic Ocean, the geological age of its basin dates as far back, at least, as the later Secondary period. The study of its animal life, as revealed in dredging, strongly confirms this, disclosing an unbroken continuity of life on the Atlantic sea-bed from the Cretaceous period to the present time; and, as Sir Charles Lyell has pointed out, in his _Principles of Geology_, the entire evidence is adverse to the idea that the Canaries, the Madeiras, and the Azores, are surviving fragments of a vast submerged island, or continuous area of the adjacent continent. There are, indeed, undoubted indications of volcanic action; but they furnish evidence of local upheaval, not of the submergence of extensive continental areas.

But it is an easy, as well as a pleasant pastime, to evolve either a camel or a continent out of the depths of one's inner consciousness. To such fanciful speculators, the lost Atlantis will ever offer a tempting basis on which to find their unsubstantial creations. Mr. H. H. Bancroft, when alluding to the subject in his _Native Races of the Pacific States_, refers to forty-two different works for notices and speculations concerning Atlantis. The latest advocacy of the idea of an actual island-continent of the mid-Atlantic, literally engulfed in the ocean, within a period authentically embraced by historical tradition, is to be found in its most popular form in Mr. Ignatius Donnelly's _Atlantis, the Antediluvian World_. By him, as by Abbé Brasseur, the concurrent opinions of the highest authorities in science, that the main features of the Atlantic basin have not changed within any recent geological period, are wholly ignored. To those, therefore, who attach any value to scientific evidence, such speculations present no serious claims on their study. There is, indeed, an idea favored by certain students of science, who carry the spirit of nationality into regions ordinarily regarded as lying outside of any sectional pride, that, geologically speaking, America is the older continent. It may at least be accepted as beyond dispute, that that continent and the great Atlantic basin intervening between it and Europe are alike of geological antiquity which places the age of either entirely apart from all speculations affecting human history. But such fancies are wholly superfluous. The idea of intercourse between the Old and the New World before the fifteenth century, passed from the region of speculation to the domain of historical fact, when the publication of the _Antiquitates Americanæ_ and the _Grönland's Historiske Mindesmærker_, by the antiquaries of Copenhagen, adduced contemporary authorities, and indisputably genuine runic inscriptions, in proof of the visits of the Northmen to Greenland and the mainland of North America, before the close of the tenth century.

The idea of pre-Columbian intercourse between Europe and America is thus no novelty. What we have anew to consider is: whether, in its wider aspect, it is more consistent with probability than the revived notion of a continent engulfed in the Atlantic Ocean. The earliest students of American antiquities turned to Phœnicia, Egypt, or other old-world centers of early civilization, for the source of Mexican, Peruvian, and Central American art or letters; and, indeed, so long as the unity of the human race remained unquestioned, some theory of a common source for the races of the Old and the New World was inevitable. The idea, therefore, that the new world that Columbus revealed, was none other than the long-lost Atlantis, is one that has probably suggested itself independently to many minds. References to America have, in like manner, been sought for in obscure allusions of Herodotus, Seneca, Pliny, and other classical writers, to islands or continents in the ocean which extended beyond the western verge of the world as known to them. That such allusions should be vague, was inevitable. If they had any foundation in knowledge by elder generations of this western hemisphere, the tradition had come down to them by the oral transmissions of centuries; while their knowledge of their eastern hemisphere was limited and very imperfect. "The Cassiterides, from which tin is brought"—assumed to be the British Isles,—were known to Herodotus only as uncertainly located islands of the Atlantic of which he had no direct information. When Assuryuchurabal, the founder of the palace at Nimrud, conquered the people who lived on the banks of the Orontes from the confines of Hamath to the sea, the spoils obtained from them included one hundred talents of _anna_or tin; and the same prized metal is repeatedly named in cuneiform inscriptions. The people trading in tin, supposed to be identical to the Shirutana, were the merchants of the world before Tyre assumed her place as chief among the merchant princes of the sea. Yet already, in the time of Joshua, she was known as "the strong city, Tyre." "Great Zidon" also is so named, along with her, when Joshua defines the bounds of the tribe of Asher, extending to the sea-coast; and is celebrated by Homer for its works of art. The Seleucia, or Cilicia, of the Greeks, was an attempted restoration of the ancient seaport of the Shirutana, which may have been an emporium of Khita merchandise; as it was, undoubtedly, an important place of shipment for the Phœnicians in their overland trade from the valley of the Euphrates. One favored etymology of Britain, as the name of the islands whence tin, was brought, is _barat-anna_, assumed to have been applied to them by that ancient race of merchant princes: the Cassiterides being the later Aryan equivalent, Gr. κασσίτερος, Sansk. _kastira_.

In primitive centuries, when ancient maritime races thus held supremacy in the Mediterranean Sea, voyages were undoubtedly made far into the Atlantic Ocean. The Phœnicians, who of all the nations settled on its shores lay among the remotest from the outlying ocean, habitually traded with settlements on the Atlantic. They colonized the western shores of the Mediterranean at a remote period; occupied numerous favorable trading posts on the bays and headlands of the Euxine, as well as of Sicily and others of the larger islands; and passed beyond the straits, effected settlements along the coasts of Europe and Africa. According to Strabo (i. 48), they had factories beyond the Pillars of Hercules in the period immediately succeeding the Trojan war: an era which yearly becomes for us less mythical, and to which may be assigned the great development of the commercial prosperity of Tyre. The Phœnicians were then expanding their trading enterprise, and extending explorations to command the remotest available sources of wealth. The trade of Tarshish was for Phœnicia what that of the East has been to England in modern centuries. The Tartessus, on which the Arabs of Spain subsequently conferred the name of the

Guadalquivir, afforded ready access to a rich mining district; and also formed the center of valuable fisheries of tunny and muræna. Using its navigable waters, along with those of the Guadiana, Phœnician traders were able to penetrate far inland; and the colonies established at their mouths furnished fresh starting points for adventurous exploration along the Atlantic seaboard. They derived much at least of the tin, which was an important object of traffic, from the mines of north-west Spain, and Cornwall; though, doubtless, both the tin of the Cassiterides and amber from the Baltic were also transported by overland routes to the Adriatic and the mouth of the Rhone. It was a Phœnician expedition that, in the reign of Pharaoh Necho, B.C. 611-605, after the decline of that great maritime power, accomplished the feat of circumnavigating Africa by way of the Red Sea. Hanno, a Carthaginian, not only guided the Punic fleet around the parts of Libya that border the Atlantic, but has been credited with reaching the Indian Ocean by the same route as that which Vasco de Gama successfully followed in 1497. The object of Hanno's expedition, as stated in the _Periplus_, was to found Libby-Phœnician cities beyond the Pillars of Hercules. How far south his voyage extended along the African coast is a matter of conjecture or disputed interpretation; for the original work is lost. It is sufficient for our purpose to know that he did pursue the same route which led in a later century to the discovery of Brazil. Aristotle applies the name of "Antilla" to a Carthaginian discovery; and Diodorus Siculus assigns to the Carthaginians the knowledge of an island in the ocean, the secret of which they reserved to themselves, as a refuge to which they could withdraw, should fate ever compel them to desert their African homes. It is far from improbable that we may identify this obscure island with one of the Azores, which lie 800 miles from the coast of Portugal. Neither Greek nor Roman writers make another reference to them; but the discovery of numerous Carthaginian coins at Corvo, the extreme north-westerly island of the group, leaves little room to doubt that they were visited by Punic voyagers. There is therefore nothing extravagant in the assumption that we have here the "Antilla" mentioned by Aristotle. While the Carthaginian oligarchy ruled, naval adventure was still encouraged; but the maritime era of the Mediterranean belongs to more ancient centuries. The Greeks were inferior in enterprise to the Phœnicians; while the Romans were essentially unmaritime, and the revival of the old adventurous spirit with the rise of the Venetian and Genoese republics was due to the infusion of fresh blood from the great northern home of the sea-kings of the Baltic.

The history of the ancient world is, for us, to a large extent, the history of civilization among the nations around the Mediterranean Sea. Its name perpetuates the recognition of it from remote times as the great inland sea which kept apart and yet united, in intercourse and exchange of experience and culture, the diverse branches of the human family settled on its shores. Of the history of those nations, we only know some later chapters. Disclosures of recent years have startled us with recovered glimpses of the Khita, or Hittites, as a great power centered between the Euphrates and the Orontes, but extending into Asia Minor, and about B.C. 1200 reaching westward to the Ægean Sea. All but their name seemed to have perished, and they were known only as one among diverse Canaanitish tribes, believed to have been displaced by the Hebrew inheritors of Palestine. Yet now, as Professor Curtius has pointed out, we begin to recognize that "one of the paths by which the art and civilization of Babylonia and Assyria made their way to Greece, was along the great high-road which runs across Asia Minor"; and which the projected railway route through the valley of the Euphrates seeks to revive. For, as compared with Egypt, and the earliest nations of Eastern Asia, the Greeks were, indeed, children. It was to the Phœnicians that the ancients assigned the origin of navigation. Their skill as seamen was the subject of admiration even by the later Greeks, who owned themselves to be their pupils in seamanship, and called the pole-star, the Phœnician star. Their naval commerce is outlined in glowing rhetoric by the prophet Ezekiel. "O Tyrus, thou that art situates at the entry of the sea, a merchant of the people of many isles. Thy borders are in the midst of the seas. The inhabitants of Zidon and Arvad were thy mariners. Thy wise men, O Tyrus, were thy pilots. All the ships of the sea, with their mariners, were in thee to occupy thy merchandise." But this was spoken at the close of Phœnician history, in the last days of Tyre's supremacy.

Looking back then into the dim dawn of actual history, with whatever fresh light recent discoveries have thrown upon it: this, at least, seems to claim recognition from us, that in that remote era the eastern Mediterranean was a center of maritime enterprises, such as had no equal among the nations of antiquity. Even in the decadence of Phœnicia, her maritime skill remained unmatched. Egypt and Palestine, under their greatest rulers, recognized her as mistress of the sea; and, as has been already noted, the circumnavigation of Africa—which, when it was repeated in the fifteenth century, was considered an achievement fully equalling that of Columbus,—had long before been accomplished by Phœnician mariners. Carthage inherited the enterprise of the mother country, but never equaled her achievements. With the fall of Carthage, the Mediterranean became a mere Roman lake, over which the galleys of Rome sailed reluctantly with her armed hosts; or coasting along the shore, they "committed themselves to the sea, and loosed the rudder bands, and hoisted up the mainsail to the winds"; or again, "strake sail, and so were driven," after the blundering fashion described in the voyage of St. Paul. To such a people, the memories of Punic exploration or Phœnician enterprise, or the vague legends of an Atlantis beyond the engirdling ocean, were equally unavailing. The narrow sea between Gaul and Britain was barrier enough to daunt the boldest of them from willingly encountering the dangers of an expedition to what seemed to them another world.

Seeing then that the first steps in navigation were taken in an age lying beyond all memory, and that the oldest traditions assign its origin to the remarkable people who figure alike in early sacred and profane history—in Joshua and Ezekiel, in Dius and Menander of Ephesus, in the Homeric poems and later Greek writings,—as unequaled in their enterprise on the sea: what impediments existed in B.C. 1400 or any earlier century that did not still exist in A.D. 1400, to render intercourse between the eastern and the western hemisphere impossible? America was no further off from Tarshish in the golden age of Tyre than in that of Henry the Navigator. With the aid of literary memorials of the race of sea-rovers who carved out for themselves the Duchy of Normandy from the domain of Charlemagne's heir, and spoiled the Angles and Saxons in their island home, we glean sufficient evidence to place the fact beyond all doubt that, after discovering and colonizing Iceland and Greenland, they made their way southward to Labrador, and so, some way along the American coast. How far south their explorations extended, after being long assigned to the locality of Rhode Island, has a new exciting interest, and is still a matter of controversy. The question is reviewed on a subsequent page; but its final settlement does not, to any degree, affect the present question. Certain it is that, about A.D. 1000, when St. Olaf was introducing Christianity by a sufficiently high-handed process into the Norse fatherland, Leif, the son of Eric, the founder of the first Greenland colony, sailed from Ericsfiord, or other Greenland port, in quest of southern lands already reported to have been seen, and did land on more than one point of the North American coast. We know what the ships of those Norse rovers were: mere galleys, not larger than a good fishing smack, and far inferior to it in deck and rigging. For compass, they had only the same old "Phœnician star," which, from the birth of navigation, had guided the mariners of the ancient world over the pathless deep. The track pursued by the Northmen, from Norway to Iceland, and so to Greenland and the Labrador coast, was, doubtless, then as now, beset by fogs, so that "neither sun nor stars in many days appeared"; and they stood much more in need of compass than the sailors of the "Santa Maria," the "Pinta," and the "Nina," the little fleet with which Columbus sailed from the Andalusian port of Palos to his first discovered land of "Guanahani," variously identified among the islands of the American Archipelago. Yet, notwithstanding all the advantages of southern latitude, with its clearer skies, we have to remember that the "Santa Maria," the only decked vessel of the expedition, was stranded; and the "Pinta" and "Nina," on which Columbus and his party had to depend for their homeward voyage, were mere coasting craft, the one with a crew of thirty, and the other with twenty-four men, with only _latine_ sails. As to the compass, we perceive how little that availed, on recalling the fact that the Portuguese admiral, Pedro Alvares de Cabral, only eight years later, when following on the route of Vasco de Gama, was carried by the equatorial current so far out of his intended course that he found himself in sight of a strange land, in 10° S. lat., and so accidentally discovered Brazil and the new world of the west, not using the mariner's compass, but despite its guidance. It is thus obvious that the discovery of America would have followed as a result of the voyage of Vasco de Gama around the Cape, wholly independent of that of Columbus. What befell the Portuguese admiral of King Manoel, in A.D. 1500, was an experience that might just as readily have fallen to the lot of the Phœnician admiral of Pharaoh Necho in B.C. 600, to the Punic Hanno, or other early navigators; and may have repeatedly occurred to Mediterranean adventurers on the Atlantic in older centuries. On the news of de Cabral's discovery reaching Portugal, the King despatched the Florentine, Amerigo Vespucci, who explored the coast of South America, prepared a map of the new-found world, and thereby wrested from Columbus the honor of giving his name to the continent which he discovered.

When we turn from the myths and traditions of the Old World to those of the New, we find their traces that seem not unfairly interpretable in the American counterpart of the legend of Atlantis. The chief seat of the highest native American civilization is neither Mexico nor Peru, but Central America. The nations of the Maya stock, who inhabit Yucatan, Guatemala, and the neighboring region, were peculiarly favorably situated; and they appear to have achieved the greatest progress among the communities of Central America. They may not unfitly compare with the ancient dwellers in the valley of the Euphrates, from the grave mounds of whose buried cities we are now recovering the history of ages that had passed into oblivion before the Father of History assumed the pen. Tested indeed by intervening centuries their monuments are not so venerable; but, for America's chroniclings, they are more prehistoric than the disclosures of Assyrian mounds. The cities of Central America were large and populous, and adorned with edifices, even now magnificent in their ruins. Still more, the Mayas were a lettered people, who, like the Egyptians, recorded in elaborately sculptured hieroglyphics the formulæ of history and creed. Like them, too, they wrote and ciphered; and appear, indeed, to have employed a comprehensive system of computing time and recording dates, which, it cannot be doubted, will be sufficiently mastered to admit to the decipherment of their ancient records. The Mayas appear, soon after the Spanish Conquest, to have adopted the Roman alphabet, and employed it in recording their historical traditions and religious myths, as well as in rendering into such written characters some of the ancient national documents. Those versions of native myth and history survive, and attention is now being directed to them. The most recent contribution from this source is _The Annals of the Cakchiquels_, by Dr. D. G. Brinton, a carefully edited and annotated translation of a native legal document or _titulo_, in which, soon after the Conquest, the heir of an ancient Maya family set forth the evidence of his claim to the inheritance. Along with this may be noted another work of the same class: _Titre Généalogique des Seigneurs de Totonicapan. Traduit de l'Espagnol par M. de Charencey._ These two works independently illustrate the same great national event. In one, a prince of the Cakchiquel nation, tells of the overthrow of the Quiché power by his people; and in the other, a Quiché seignior, one of the "Lords of Totonicapan," describes it from his point of view. Both were of the same Maya stock, in what is now the State of Guatemala. Each nation had a capital adorned with temples and palaces, the splendor of which excited the wonder of the Spaniards; and both preserved traditions of the migration of their ancestors from Tula, a mythical land from which they came across the water.

Such traditions of migration meet us on many sides. Captain Cook found among the mythological traditions of Tahiti, a vague legend of a ship that came out of the ocean, and seemed to be the dim record of ancestral intercourse with the outer world. So also, the Aztecs had the tradition of the golden age of Anahuac; and of Quetzalcoatl, their instructor in agriculture, metallurgy, and the arts of government. He was of fair complexion, with long dark hair, and a flowing beard: all, characteristics foreign to their race. When his mission was completed, he set sail for the mysterious shores of Tlapallan; and on the appearance of the ships of Cortes, the Spaniards were believed to have returned with the divine instructor of their forefathers, from the source of the rising sun.

What tradition hints at, physiology confirms. The races of America differ less in physical character from those of Asia, than do the races either of Africa or Europe. The American Indian is a Mongol; and though marked diversities are traceable throughout the American continent, the range of variation is much less than in the eastern hemisphere. The western continent appears to have been peopled by repeated migrations and by diverse routes; but when we attempt to estimate any probable date for its primeval settlement, evidence wholly fails. Language proves elsewhere a safe guide. It has established beyond question some long-forgotten relationship between the Aryans of India and Persia and those of Europe; it connects the Finn and Lapp with their Asiatic forefathers; it marks the independent origin of the Basques and their priority to the oldest Aryan intruders; it links together widely diverse branches of the great Semitic family. Can language tell us of any such American affinities, or traces of Old World congeners, about either civilized Mayas and Peruvians, or to the forest and prairie races of the northern continent?

With the millions of America's colored population, of African blood, and yet speaking Aryan languages, the American comparative philologist can scarcely miss the significance of the warning that linguistic and ethnic classifications by no means necessarily imply the same thing. Nevertheless, without overlooking this distinction, the ethical significance of the evidence that comparative philology supplies cannot be slighted in any question relative to prehistoric relations between the Old World and the New. What then can philology tell us? There is one answer, at the least, which the languages of America give, that fully accords with the legend, "white with age," that told of an island-continent in the Atlantic Ocean with which the nations around the Mediterranean once held intercourse. None of them indicates any trace of immigration within the period of earliest authentic history. Those who attach significance to the references in the _Timæus_ to political relations common to Atlantis and parts of Libya and Europe; or who, on other grounds, look with favor on the idea of early intercourse between the Mediterranean and the western continent, have naturally turned to the Eskuara of the Basques. It is invariably recognized as the surviving representative of languages spoken by the Allophyliæ of Europe before the intrusion of Aryans. The forms of its grammar differ widely from those of any Semitic, or Indo-European tongue, placing it in the same class with Mongol, East African, and American languages. Here, therefore, is a tempting glimpse of possible affinities; and Professor Whitney, accordingly, remarks in his _Life and Growth of Languages_, that the Basque "forms a suitable stepping-stone from which to enter the peculiar linguistic domain of the New World since there is no other dialect of the Old World which so much resembles in structure the American languages." But this glimpse of a possible relationship has proved, thus far, illusory. In their morphological character, certain American and Asiatic languages have a common agglutinative structure, which in the former is developed into their characteristic polysynthetic attribute. With this, the Eskuarian system of affixes corresponds. But beyond the general structure, there is no such evidence of affinity, either in the vocabularies or grammar, as direct affiliation might be expected to show. Elements common to the Anglo-Americans of the nineteenth century and the Sanskrit-speaking race beyond the Indus, in the era of Alexander of Macedon, are suggested at once by the grammatical structure of their languages; whereas there is nothing in the resemblance between the Basque and any of the North American languages that are not compatible with a "stepping-stone" from Asia to America by the islands of the Pacific. The most important of all the native American languages in their bearing on this interesting inquiry—those of Central America,—are only now receiving adequate attention. Startling evidence may yet reward the diligence of students; but, so far as language furnishes any clue to the affinity of race, no American language thus far discloses such a relationship, as, for example, enabled Dr. Pritchard to suggest that the western people of Europe, to whom the Greeks gave the collective name of Κέλται, and whose languages had been assumed by all previous ethnologists as furnishing evidence that they were precursors of the Aryan immigrants, in reality, justified their classification in the same stock.

But while thus far, the evidence of language is, at best, vague and indefinite in its response to the inquiry for proof of the relationship of the races of America to those of the Old World; physiological comparisons lend no confirmation to the idea of an indigenous native race, with special affinities and adaptation to its peculiar environment, and with languages all of one class, the ramifications from a single native stem. So far as physical affinities can be relied upon, the man of America, in all his most characteristic racial diversities, is of Asiatic origin. His near approximation to the Asiatic Mongol is so manifest as to have led observers of widely different opinions in all other respects, to concur in classing both under the same great division: the Mongolian of Pickering, the American Mongolidæ of Latham, the Mongoloid of Huxley. Professor Flower, in an able discussion of the varieties of the human species, addressed the Anthropological Institute of Great Britain in 1885, unhesitatingly classes the Eskimo as the typical North Asiatic Mongol. In other American races he notes as distinctive features the characteristic form of the nasal bones, the well-developed superciliary ridge, and retreating forehead; but the resemblance is so obvious in many other respects, that he finally includes them all among the members of the Mongolian type. If, then, the American Mongol came originally from Asia, or sprung from the common stock of which the Asiatic Mongol is the typical representative, within any such period as even earliest Phœnician history would embrace, much more definite traces of affinity are to be looked for in his language than mere correspondence in the agglutination characteristic of a very widely diffused class of speech. But we, thus far, look in vain for traces of a common genealogy such as those which, on the one hand, correlate the Semitic and Aryan families of Asia and Europe with parent stocks of times anterior to history, and on the other, with ramifications of modern centuries. We have, moreover, to deal mainly with the languages of uncivilized races. To the continent north of the Gulf of Mexico, the grand civilizing art of the metallurgist remained to the last unknown; and in Mexico, it appears as a gift of recent origin, derived from Central America. The Asiatic origin of the art of Tubal-Cain has, indeed, been pretty generally assumed, both for Central and Southern America; but by mere inference. In doing so, we are carried back to some mythic Quetzalcoatl: for neither the metallurgist nor his art was introduced in recent centuries. Assuming, for the sake of argument, the dispersion of a common population of Asia and America, already familiar with the working of metals, and with architecture, sculpture, and other kindred arts, at a date coeval with the founding of Tyre, "the daughter of Sidon," what help does language give us in favor of such a postulate? We have great language groups, such as the Huron-Iroquois, extending of old from St. Lawrence to North Carolina; the Algonkin, from Hudson Bay to South Carolina; the Dakotan, from the Mississippi to the Rocky Mountains; the Athabascan, from the Eskimo frontier, within the Arctic circle, to New Mexico; and the Tinné family of languages west of the Rocky Mountains, from the Yukon and Mackenzie rivers, far south on the Pacific slope. With those, as with the more cultured languages, or rather languages of the more cultured races, of Central and Southern America, elaborate comparisons have been made with vocabularies of Asiatic languages; but the results are, at best, vague. Curious points of agreement have, indeed, been demonstrated, inviting further research; but as yet the evidence of relationship mainly rests on correspondence in structure. The agglutinative suffixes are common to the Eskimo and many American Indian tongues. Dr. H. Rink describes the polysynthetic process in the Eskimo language as founded on radical words, to which additional or imperfect words, or affixes, are attached; and on the inflection, which, for transitive verbs, indicates subject as well as object, likewise by addition. But, while Professor Flower unhesitatingly characterizes the Eskimo as belonging to the typical North Asiatic Mongols; he, at the same time, speaks of them as almost as perfectly isolated in their Arctic home "as an island population." Nevertheless, the same structure is common to their language and those of the great North American families already named. All alike present, in an exaggerated form, the characteristic structure of the Ural-Altaic or Turanian group of Asiatic languages.

Race-type corresponds to the Old and New World. A comparison of languages using the vocabularies of the two continents yields no such correspondence. All the more, therefore, is the American student of comparative philology stimulated to investigate the significance of the polysynthetic characteristic found to pertain to so many—though by no means to all—of the languages of this continent. The relationship which it suggests to the agglutinative languages of Asia furnishes a subject of investigation not less interesting to American students, like of the science of language, and of the whole comprehensive questions which anthropology embraces, than the relations of the Romance languages of Europe to the parent Latin; or of Latin itself, and all the Aryan languages, ancient and modern, not only to Sanskrit and Zend, but to the indeterminate stock which furnished the parent roots, the grammatical forms, and that whole class of words still recognizable as the common property of the whole Aryan family. Sanskrit was a dead language three thousand years ago; the English language, as such, cannot claim to have endured much more than fourteen centuries, yet both partake of the same common property of numerals and familiar terms existing under certain modifications in Sanskrit, Greek, Latin, Slavonic, Celtic, German, Anglo-Saxon, and in all the Romance languages. Thus far the American philologist has been unable to show any such genealogical relationship pervading the native languages, or to recover specific evidence of affinities to languages, and so to races of other continents. There are, indeed, linguistic families, such as some already referred to, indicating a common descent among widely dispersed tribes; but this has its chief interest in another aspect of the question.

Professor Max Müller has drawn attention to the tendency of the languages of America towards an endless multiplication of distinct dialects. Those again have been grouped by the synthetic process of Hervas into eleven families: seven for the northern continent, and four for South America. But we are as yet only on the threshold of this important branch of research. In two papers contributed by M. Lucien Adam to the _Congrès International des Americanistes_, he gives the results of a careful examination of sixteen languages of North and South America; and concludes that they belong to several independent families as essentially distinct as they would have been "had there been primitively several human pairs." Dr. Brinton, one of the highest authorities on any question connected with Native American languages, contributed a paper to the _American Antiquarian_ (Jan. 1886), "On the Study of the Nahuatl Language." This language, which is popularly known as Aztec, he strongly commends to the study of American philologists. It is one of the most completely organized Indian languages, has a literature of considerable extent and variety, and is still in use by upwards of half a million people. It is from this area, southward through Central America, and in the great seat of native South American civilization, that we can alone hope to recover direct evidence of ancient intercourse between the Old and the New World. But, here again, the complexities of language seem to grow apace. In Dr. Brinton's _Notes on the Mangue, an extinct Language formerly spoken in Nicaragua_, he states, as a result of his later studies, that the belief that he once entertained of some possible connection between this dialect and the Aymara of Peru, has not been confirmed on further examination. This, therefore, tends to sustain the prevailing opinion of scholars that there is no direct affiliation between the languages of North and South America. All this is suggestive of an idea, such as that which Agassiz favored in his system of natural provinces of the animal world, about different types of man, on which he based the conclusion that the diverse varieties of American man originated in various centers, and had been distributed from them over the entire continent; or we must assume immigration from different foreign centers. Accepting the latter as the more tenable proposition, I long ago sketched a scheme of immigration such as seemed to harmonize with the suggestive, though imperfect evidence. This assumed the earliest current of population, in its progress from a supposed Asiatic cradleland, to have spread through the islands of the Pacific, and reached the South American continent before any excess of the population had diffused itself into the inhospitable northern steppes of Asia. By an Atlantic oceanic migration, another wave of the population occupied the Canaries, Madeiras, and the Azores, and so passed to the Antilles, Central America, and probably by the Cape Verdes, or, guided by the more southern equatorial current, to Brazil. Latest of all, Behring Strait and the North Pacific Islands may have become the highway for a migration by which certain striking diversities among nations of the northern continent, including the conquerors of the Mexican plateau, are most easily accounted for.

It is not necessary to include in the question here discussed, the more comprehensive one of the existence of man in America contemporary with the great extinct animals of the Quaternary Period; though the acknowledged affinities of Asiatic and American anthropology, taken in connection with the remoteness of any assignable period for migration from Asia to the American continent, renders it far from improbable that the latest oscillations of land may here also have exercised an influence. The present soundings of Behring Strait, and the bed of the sea extending southward to the Aleutian Islands, are entirely in accord with the assumption of a former continuity of land between Asia and America. The idea which the speculations of Darwin, founded on his observations during the voyage of the 'Beagle' gave rise, to continuous subsidence of the Pacific Ocean, and also favored the probability of greater insular facilities for trans-oceanic migration at the supposed period of the peopling of America from Asia. But more recent explorations, and especially those connected with the 'Challenger' expedition, fail to confirm the old theory of the origin of the coral islands of the Pacific; and in any view of the case, we must be content to study the history of existing races, alike of Europe and America, apart from questions relating to palæocosmic man. If the vague legend of the lost Atlantis embodies any trace of remotest historical tradition, it belongs to a modern era compared with the men either of the European drift or the post-glacial deposits of Delaware and the auriferous gravels of California. When the resort is had to comparative philology, it is manifest that we must be content to deal with a more recent era than contemporaries of the Mastodon, and their congeners of Europe's Mammoth and Reindeer periods, even though the modern representatives of the latter have been sought within the American Arctic circle.

Such evidence as a comparison of languages thus far supplies, lends more countenance to the idea of migration through the islands of the Pacific, than to such a route from the Mediterranean as is implied in any significance attached to the legend of Atlantis. As to the Behring Strait route, present ethnology and philology point rather to an overflow of Arctic American population into Asia. Gallatin was the first to draw attention to certain analogies in the structure of Polynesian and American languages, as deserving of investigation; and pointed out the peculiar mode of expressing the tense, mood, and voice of the verb, by affixed particles, and the value given to place over time, as indicated in the predominant locative verbal form. Such is to be looked for with greater probability among the languages of South America; but the substitution of affixed particles for inflections, especially in expressing the direction of action of the speaker, is common to the Polynesian and the Oregon languages, and has analogies in the Cherokee. The distinction between the inclusive and exclusive pronoun _we_, according as it means "you and I," or "they and I," etc., is as characteristic of the Maori as of the Ojibway. Other observations of more recent date have still further tended to countenance the recognition of elements common to the languages of Polynesia and America, and so to point to migration by the Pacific to the western continent.

But this idea of migration through the islands of the Pacific receives curious confirmation from another source. In an ingenious paper on "The Origin of Primitive Money," originally read at the meeting of the British Association at Montreal in 1884, Mr. Horatio Hale shows that there is good reason for believing that the most ancient currency in China consisted of disks and slips of tortoise shell. The fact is stated in the great Chinese encyclopædia of Emperor Kang-he, who reigned in the early years of the eighteenth century; and the Chinese annalists assert that metal coins have been in use from the time of Fuh-he, about B.C. 2950. Without attempting to determine the specific accuracy of Chinese chronology, it is sufficient to note here that the most ancient form of Chinese copper cash is the disk, perforated with a square hole, to admit the coins being strung together. This, which corresponds in form to the large perforated shell disks, or native currency of the Indians of California, and with specimens recovered from ancient mounds, Mr. Hale regards as the later imitation in the metal of the original Chinese shell money. A similar shell currency, as he shows, is in use among many islanders of the Pacific; and he traces it from the Loo-Choo Islands, across the vast archipelago, through many island groups, to California; and then overland, with the aid of numerous disclosures from ancient mounds to the Atlantic coast, where the Indians of Long Island were long noted for its manufacture in the later form of wampum. "The natives of Micronesia," says Mr. Hale, who, it will be remembered, records the results of personal observation, "in character, usages, and language, resemble a certain extent the nations of the southern and eastern Pacific groups, which are included in the designation of Polynesia, but with some striking differences, which careful observers have ascribed, with great probability, to influences from north-eastern Asia. They are noted for their skill in navigation. They have well-rigged vessels, exceeding sixty feet in length. They sail by the stars, and are accustomed to taking long voyages." To such voyagers, the Pacific presents no more formidable impediments to oceanic enterprise than did the Atlantic to the Northmen of the tenth century.

Throughout the same archipelago, modern exploration is rendering us familiar with examples of remarkable stone structures and colossal sculptured figures, such as those from Easter Island now in the British Museum. Rude as they undoubtedly are, they are highly suggestive of an affinity to the megalithic sculptures and cyclopean masonry of Peru. Monuments of this class were noted long ago by Captain Beechy on some of the islands nearest the coasts of Chili and Peru. Since then the megalithic area has been extended by their discovery in other island groups lying on the continent of Asia.

Another subsidiary class of evidence of a different kind, long since noted by me, gives additional confirmation to this recovered trail of ancient migration through the islands of the Pacific to the American continent. The practice to which the Flathead Indians of Oregon and

British Columbia owe their name, the compressed skulls from Peruvian cemeteries, and the widely diffused evidence of the prevalence of such artificial malformation among many American tribes, combine to indicate it as one of the most characteristic American customs. Yet the evidence is abundant which shows it not only as a practice among rude Asiatic Mongol tribes of primitive centuries, but proves that it was still in use among the Huns and Avars who contended with the Barbarians from the Baltic for the spoils of the decaying Roman empire. Nor was it merely common to tribes of both continents. It furnishes another link in the chain of evidence of ancient migration from Asia to America; as is proved by its practice in some of the islands of the Pacific, as described by Dr. Pickering,[2] and since abundantly confirmed by the forms of Kanaka skulls. By following up the traces of this strange custom, perpetuated among the tribes on the Pacific coasts both of Northern and Southern America to our day, we thus once more retrace the steps of ancient wanderers, and are carried back to centuries when the Macrocephaly of the Euxine attracted the observant eye of Hippocrates, and became familiar to Strabo, Pliny, and Pomponius Mela.

But the wanderings among the insular races of the Pacific are not limited to such remote eras. Later changes are also recorded by other evidence. The direct relationship of existing Polynesian languages is not Mongol but Malay, but this is the intrusive element of a time long after the growth of characteristic features which still perpetuate traces of Polynesian and American affinities. The number and diversity of the languages of the continent of America, and their essentially native vocabularies, prove that the latter has been in a prolonged process of development, free from contact with languages that appear to have been still modeling themselves according to the same plan of thought in many scattered islands of the Pacific.

The remarkable amount of culture in the languages of some of the barbarous nations of North America, traceable, apparently, to the important part which the orator played in their deliberative assemblies, has not unnaturally excited surprise: but in any attempt to recover the history of the New World by the aid of philology we must deal with the languages of its civilized races. Among those, the Nahuatl or Aztec has been appealed to, and the Mayas have been noted as a lettered people whose hieroglyphic records, and later transcripts of written documents, are now the object of intelligent investigation both by European and American philologists. The Maya language strikingly contrasts, in its soft, vocalic forms, with the languages of nations immediately to the north of its native area. It is that which, according to Stephens, was affirmed to be still spoken by a living race in a region beyond the Great Sierra, extending to Yucatan and the Mexican Gulf. Others among the cultured native languages which seem to invite special study are the Aymara and the Quichua. Of these, the latter was the classical language of South America, wherein, according to its native historians, the Peruvian chroniclers and poets incorporated the national legends. It may be described as having occupied a place under Inca rule analogous to that of the Norman French in England from the eleventh to the thirteenth century. To those ancient, cultured languages of the seats of indigenous civilization, and with a literature of their own, attention is now happily directed. The students of American ethnology begin to realize that the buried mounds of Assyria are not richer in discoveries relative to the ancient history of Asia than are the monuments, the hieroglyphic records, and the languages of Central America and Peru, about a native social life which long flourished as a product of their West. To this occidental Assyria, we have to look for an answer to many inquiries, especially interesting to the intrusive occupants of the western continent. If its architecture and sculpture, and the hieroglyphic records with which they are enriched, are modifications of a prehistoric Asiatic civilization, it is here that the evidence is to be looked for; and if the arts of the sculptor and architect were brought to the continent of America by wanderers from an Asiatic fatherland, then those of the potter and the metallurgist will also prove to be an inheritance from the old Asiatic hive of the nations.

From the evidence thus far adduced it appears that ethnically the American is Mongol, and by the agglutinative element in many of the native languages may be classed as Turanian. The Finnic hypothesis of Rask, however much modified by later reconsideration of the question of the origin of the Aryans, as well as the European melanochroic Metis of Huxley, pertains to a prehistoric era of which the Finns and the Basques are assumed to be survivals; and to that elder era, rather than to any date within the remotest limits of authentic history, the languages of America seem to refer us in the search for any common origin with those of the eastern hemisphere. But a zealous comparative philologist, already referred to, has sought linguistic traces of the relationship between the Old and the New World which, if confirmed, would better harmonize with the traditions of intercourse between the maritime nations of the eastern Mediterranean and a continent lying outside of the Pillars of Hercules. In his investigations, he aims at determining the relations of the Aztec or Nahuatl culture and language to those of Asia. Humboldt long ago claimed for much of the former an Old World derivation. It seems premature to attempt to deduce any comprehensive results from the meager data thus far gathered. But the author of _The Khita and Khita-Peruvian Epoch_, in tracing the progress of his Sumerian race, assigns 4000 years since their settlement in Babylonia and India. In like manner, on the assumption of their migration from a common Asiatic center, which the division of Western and Eastern Sumerian in pronouns and other details is thought to indicate, Peru, it is conceived, may have been reached by a migratory wave of earlier movement, from 4000 to 5000 years ago. Mr. Hyde Clarke indeed conceives that it is quite a within compass that the same great wave of migration that passed over India and Babylonia, continued to propagate its centrifugal force, and that by its means Peru was reached within the last 3000 years. But, whatever intercourse may have then been carried on between the Old and the New World, it must be obvious, on mature reflection, that so recent a date for the peopling of South America from Asia is as little reconcilable with the very remote traces of linguistic affinity thus far adduced, as it is with any fancied relationship with a lost Atlantis of the elder world. The enduring affinities of long-parted languages of the Old World tell a very different tale. With the comparative philologist, as with the archæologist, time is more and more coming to be recognized as an all-important factor.

But, leaving the estimate of centuries out of consideration, in the research into the origin of the peculiar native civilization of America here referred to, the recently deciphered Akkad is accepted as the typical language of the Sumerian class. This is assumed to have started from High Asia and to have passed on to Babylonia; while another branch diffused itself by India and Indo-China, and thence, by way of the islands of the Pacific, reached America.

Hence, in an illustrative table of Sumerian words arranged under four heads, as Western, Indo-Chinese, Peruvian, and Mexican, etc., it is noted that "while in some cases a root may be traced throughout, it will be seen that more commonly the western and American roots or types, cross in the Indo-Chinese region." But another and older influence, related to the Agaw of the Nile region, is also traced in the Guarani, Omega, and other languages of South America, indicating evidence of more remote relations with the Old World, and with the African continent. This is supposed to have been displaced by a Sumerian migration by which the Aymara domination was established in Peru, and the Maya element was introduced into Yucatan. Those movements are assumed to belong to an era of civilization, during which the maritime enterprise of the Pacific may have been carried on upon a scale unknown to the most adventurous of modern Malay navigators, notwithstanding the essentially maritime character by which the race is still distinguished. All this implies that the highway to the Pacific was familiar to both continents; hence a second migration is recognized, in certain linguistic relations, between the Siamese and other languages of Indo-China, and the Quichua and Aztec of Peru and Mexico. But the problem of the origin of the races of the western continent, and the sources of its native civilization, is still in that preliminary stage in which the accumulation of materials on which future induction may be based is of more value than the most comprehensive generalizations.

The vastness of the American twin continents, with their Atlantic and Pacific seaboard reaching from the Arctic well-nigh to the Antarctic circle, furnishes a tempting stimulus to theories of migration on the grandest scale, and the assumption of comprehensive schemes of international relation in prehistoric centuries. But they are not more substantial than the old legend of Atlantis. The best that can be said of them is that here, at any rate, are lines of research in the prosecution of which American ethnologists may employ their learning and acumen encouraged by the hope of yet revealing a past not less marvelous, and possessing a more personal interest, than all which geology has recovered from the testimony of the rocks. But before such can be more than dimly guessed at, the patient diligence of many students will be needed to accumulate the needful materials. Nor can we afford to delay the task. The Narraganset Bible, the work of Eliot, the apostle of the Indians, is the memorial of a race that has perished; while other nations and languages have disappeared since his day, with no such invaluable record of their character. Mr. Horatio Hale published in the _Proceedings of the American Philosophical Society_, in 1883, a paper on the "Tutelo Tribe and Language," derived from Nikonha, the last survivor of a once powerful tribe of North Carolina. To Dr. Brinton, we owe the recent valuable notes on the Mangue, another extinct language. On the North-western Canadian prairies, the buffalo has disappeared, and the Indian must follow. On all hands, we are called upon to work diligently while it is yet time, to accumulate the materials out of which the history of the western hemisphere is to be evolved.

It accords with the idea of Polynesian genealogy, that indications suggestive of grammatical affinity have been noted in languages of South America, in their mode of expressing the tense of the verb; in the formation of causative, reciprocal, potential, and locative verbs by affixes; and in the general system of compound word structure. The incorporation of the particle with the verbal root appears to embody the germ of the more comprehensive American holophrases. Such affinities point to others more markedly Asiatic; for analogies recognized between the languages of the Deccan and those of the Polynesian group about the determinative significance of the formative particles on the verbal root, reappear in some of the characteristic peculiarities of American languages. On this subject, the Rev. Richard Garnett remarked, in a communication to the Philological Society, that most of the native American languages of which we have definite information, bear a general analogy alike to the Polynesian family and the languages of the Deccan, in their methods of distinguishing the various modifications of time; and he adds: "We may venture to affirm, in general terms, that a South American verb is constructed precisely as those in the Tamil and other languages of Southern India; consisting, like them, of a verbal root, a second element defining the time of the action, and a third denoting the subject or person."

So far it becomes apparent that the evidence, derived alike from language and other sources, points to the isolation of the American continent through unnumbered ages. The legend of the lost Atlantis is true in this, if in nothing else, that it relegates the knowledge of the world beyond the Atlantic, by the maritime races of the Mediterranean, to a time already of hoar antiquity in the age of Socrates, or even of Solon. But at a greatly later date, the Caribbean Sea was scarcely more a mystery to the dwellers on the shores of the Ægean, than was the Baltic or the North Sea. Herodotus, indeed, expressly affirms his disbelief in "a river, called by the barbarians, Eridanus, which flows into a northern sea, and from which there is a report that amber is wont to come." Nevertheless, we learn from him of Greek traders exchanging personal ornaments and woven stuff for the furs and amber of the North. They ascended the Dneiper as far as Gerrhos, a trading post, forty days' journey inland; and the tokens of their presence there have been recovered in modern times. Not only hoards of Greek coins, minted in the fifth century B.C., but older golden griffins of Assyrian workmanship have been recovered during the present century, near Bromberg in Posen, and at Kyiv on the Dneiper. As also, afar on the most northern island of the Azores, hoards of Carthaginian coins have revealed traces of the old Punic voyager there; if still more ancient voyagers from Sidon, Tyre, or Seleucia, did find their way in some forgotten century to lands that lay beyond the waste of waters which seemed to engirdle their world: similar evidence may yet be forthcoming among the traces of ancient native civilization in Central or Southern America.

But also the carving of names and dates, and other graphic memorials of the passing wayfarer is no mere modern custom. When the sites of Greenland settlements of the Northmen of the tenth century were discovered in our day, the runic inscriptions left no room for doubt as to their former presence there. By like evidence, we learn of them in southern lands, from their runes still legible on the marble lion of the Piræus, since transported to its later site in the arsenal of Venice. At Maeshowe in Orkney, in St. Molio's Cave on the Clyde, at Kirk Michael in the Isle of Man, and on many a rock and stone by the Baltic, the sea-rovers from the north have left enduring evidence of their wanderings. So was it with the Roman? From the Moray Firth to the Libyan desert, and from the Iberian shore to the Syrian valleys, sepulchral, legionary, and mythological inscriptions, as well as coins, medals, pottery, and works of art, mark the footprints of the masters of the world. In Italy, itself Perusinian, Eugubine, Etruscan, and Greek inscriptions tell the story of a succession of races in that beautiful peninsula. It was the same, through all the centuries of Hellenic intellectual rule, back to the unrivaled inscription at Abu Simbel. This was cut, says Dr. Isaac Taylor,[3] "when what we call Greek history can hardly be said to have commenced: two hundred years before Herodotus, the Father of History, had composed his work; a century before Athens began to rise to power. More ancient even than the epoch assigned to Solon, Thales, and the seven wise men of Greece: it must be placed in the half-legendary period at which the laws of Dracon are said to have been enacted";—the period from which the legend of Atlantis was professedly derived. Yet there the graven characters perpetuate their authentic bit of history, legible to this day, of the son of Theories, sailing with his company up the Nile, when King Psamatichos came to Elephantine. So it is with Egyptians, Assyrians, Phœnicians, and with the strange forgotten Hittites, whose vast empire has vanished from the world's memory. The lion of the Piræus, with its graven runes, is a thing of yesterday, compared with the inscribed lion from Marash, with its Hittite hieroglyphs, now in the museum at Constantinople; for the Hittite capital, Ketesh, was captured by the Egyptian Sethos, B.C. 1340. All but the name of these once powerful people seemed to have perished. Yet the inscribed stones, by which they were to be restored to their place in history, remained, awaiting the interpretation of an enlightened age.

If then, traces of the lost Atlantis are ever to be recovered in the New World, it must be by some indubitable memorial of a like kind. Old as the legend may be, it is seen that literal graphic memorials—Assyrian, Phœnician, Khita, Egyptian, and Greek,—remain to tell of times even beyond the epoch assigned to Solon. The antiquaries of New England have sought in vain for runic memorials of the Northmen of the tenth century; and the diligence of less trustworthy explorers for traces of ancient records has been stimulated to excess, throughout the North American continent, with results little more creditable to their honesty than their judgment. What some chance disclosure may yet reveal, who can presume to guess? But thus far it appears to be improbable that within the area north of the Gulf of Mexico, evidence of the presence of Phœnician, Greek, or other ancient historic race will now be found. Certain it is that, whatever transient visits may have been paid to North America by representatives of Old World progress, no long-matured civilization, whether of native or foreign origin, has existed there. Through all the centuries of which definite history has anything to tell, it has remained a world apart, secure in its isolation, with languages, arts, and customs essentially native in character. The nations of the Maya stock appear to have made the greatest progress in the civilization of all the communities of Central America. They dwelt in cities adorned with costly structures dedicated to the purposes of religion and the state; and had a political government, and forms of social organization, to all appearance, the slow growth of many generations. They had, also, a well-matured system of chronology; and have left behind them graven and written records, analogous to those of ancient Egypt, which still await decipherment. Whether this culture was pure of native growth or had its origin from the germs of an Old World civilization, can only be determined when its secrets have been fully mastered. The region is even now very partially explored. The students of American ethnology and archæology are only awakening to some adequate sense of its importance. But there appears to have been the center of a Native American civilization whence light was slowly radiating on either hand, before the vandals of the Spanish Conquest quenched it in blood. The civilization of Mexico was but a borrowed reflex of that of Central America, and its picture-writing is a very inferior imitation of the ideography of the Maya hieroglyphics.

A tendency manifests itself anew to trace the metallurgy, the letters, the astronomical science, and whatever else marks the quickening into the intellectual life of this American leading race, to an Asiatic or other Old World origin. The point, however, is by no means established; nor can any reason be shown why the human intellect might not be started on the same course in Central America, as in Mesopotamia or the valley of the Nile. If we assume the primary settlement of Central America by expeditions systematically carried on under the auspices of some ancient maritime power of the Mediterranean, or of an early seat of Iberian or Libyan civilization, then they would, undoubtedly, transplant the arts of their old home to the New World. But, on the more probable supposition of wanderers, either by the Atlantic or the Pacific, being landed on its shores, and becoming the undesigned settlers of the continent, it is otherwise; and the probabilities are still further diminished if we conceive of ocean wanderers from island to island of the Pacific, at length reaching the shores of the remote continent after the traditions of their Asiatic fatherland had faded from the memory of later generations. The condition of metallurgy as practiced by the Mexicans and Peruvians exhibited none of the matured phases of an inheritance from remote generations but partook rather of the tentative characteristics of immature native art.

We are prone to overestimate the facilities by which the arts of civilization may be transplanted to remote regions. It is not greatly more difficult to conceive of the rediscovery of some of the essential elements of human progress than to believe in the transference of them from the eastern to the western hemisphere by wanderers from either Europe or Asia. Take the average type of emigrants, such as are annually landed by thousands at New York. They come from the most civilized countries in Europe. Yet, how few among them all could be relied upon for any such intelligent comprehension of metallurgy, if left entirely to their resources, as to be found able to turn the mineral wealth of their new home to practical account; or for astronomical science, such as would enable them to construct a calendar, and start afresh a systematic chronology. As to letters, the picture-writing of the Aztecs was the same in principle as the rude art of the northern Indians; and I cannot conceive of any reason for rejecting the assumption of its native origin as an intellectual triumph achieved by the labors of many generations. Every step is still traceable, from the rude picturings on the Indian's grave-post or rock inscription, to the systematic ideographs of Palenque or Copan. Hieroglyphics, as the natural outgrowth of pictorial representation, must always have a general family likeness; but all attempts to connect the civilization of Central and Southern America with that of Egypt fail, so soon as a comparison is instituted between the Egyptian calendar and any of the native American systems of recording dates and computing time. The vague year of 365 days, and the corrected solar year, with the great Sothic Cycle of 1460 years, so intimately interwoven with the religious system and historical chronology of the

Egyptians, abundantly prove the correction of the Egyptian calendar by accumulated experience, at a date long anterior to the resort of the Greek astronomer, Thales, to Egypt. At the close of the fifteenth century, the Aztecs had learned to correct their calendar to solar time; but their cycle was one of only fifty-two years. The Peruvians also had their recurrent religious festivals, connected with the adjustment of their sacred calendar to solar time; but the geographical position of Peru, with Quito, its holy city, lying immediately under the equator, greatly simplified the process by which they regulated their religious festivals by the solstices and equinoxes. The facilities which their equatorial position afforded for determining the few indispensable periods in their calendar were, indeed, a doubtful advantage, for they removed all stimulus to progress. The Mexican calendar is the most remarkable evidence of the civilization attained by that people. Humboldt unhesitatingly connected it with the ancient science of south-eastern Asia. But instead of its exhibiting any such inevitable accumulation of error as that which gave so peculiar a character to the historical chronology of the Egyptians, its computation differed less from true solar time than the unreformed Julian calendar which the Spaniards had inherited from pagan Rome. But though this suffices to show that the civilization of Mexico was of no great antiquity, it only accords with other evidence of its borrowed character. The Mexicans stood in the same relation to Central America as the Northern Barbarians of the third and fourth century did to Italy, and the intruding Spaniard nipped their germ of borrowed civilization in the bud. So long as the search for evidence either of a native or intruded civilization is limited to the northern continent of America, it is equivalent to an attempt to recover the traces of Greek and Roman civilization in transalpine Europe. The Mexican calendar stone is no more than the counterpart of some stray Greek or Roman tablet beyond the Alps; or rather, perhaps, of some Mæsogothic product of borrowed art.

Therefore, we must wait for careful research of Central America before drawing any firm conclusions about the untold history of the New World. Numerous inscriptions are present on the sculptured tablets of Palenque, Quiriqua, Chichen Itza, and Uxmal as well as on the enormous sculptures at Copan and other historic sites. These texts are waiting to be deciphered by the next Young or Champollion of American paleography.

A lettered race that shared the same written characters and a common civilization formerly occupied the entire area. We can confidently anticipate the discovery of some graphic memorial of the messenger, confirming the recurrent legends of bearded white men who came from beyond the sea and introduced the arts of civilization. If they owed the great invention of letters to some apostle from the Mediterranean, which, as Bacon says, "as ships, pass through the vast seas of time, and make ages so distant to participate of the wisdom, illuminations, and inventions, the one of the other:" It cannot be that the pre-Columbian discoveries of the Northmen's graphic runes have established beyond all doubt the existence of their Egyptian, Assyrian, Hittite, Phoenician, and other most ancient races, but that there is not a single remnant of the Mediterranean wanderers to the lost Atlantis. An engraving of a portion of a purported Phoenician inscription can be seen in Humboldt's "Researches." A Franciscan monk named Ranson Bueno reproduced it after finding a piece of granite in a cavern in the mountains between the Orinoco and the Amazon. Humboldt noticed several similarities to the Phoenician script in it. However, we must keep in mind how crudely transcribed Phnician characters are; as for their transcriber, it is likely that he had no prior understanding of Phoenicians.

Although he had duplicated it extremely meticulously, Humboldt wrote of him, "The pious monk seemed to be but little bothered about this fake inscription."

So the future is where the lost city of Atlantis is still. The earlier investigations of the monuments and prehistoric relics on the American continent seemed to be able to prove beyond a doubt that its civilization originated from native sources.

Continuous steps seem to have been taken by an American man to develop for himself the same wondrous invention of letters that ancient legend ascribed to Thoth or Mercury, or, in a less mythical form, to the Phoenician Cadmus, from quipu and wampum, pictured grave-post and buffalo robe, to the most finished hieroglyphs of Copan or Palenque.

Nor has the generally accepted assumption of a foreign origin for American metallurgy been placed as yet on any substantial basis. Gold, as I believe, was everywhere the first metal wrought. The bright nugget tempted the savage, with whom personal ornaments precede dress. It was readily fashioned into any desired shape. The same is true, though to a less degree, of copper; and wherever, as on the American continent, native copper abounds, the next step in metallurgy is to be anticipated. With the discovery of the economic use of the metals, an all-important step had been achieved, leading to the fashioning of useful tools, architecture, sculpture, pictorial ornamentation, and so on ideography. The facilities for all this were, at least, as abundant in Central and Southern America as in Egypt. The progress was, doubtless, slow; but when the Neolithic age began to yield to that of the metallurgist, the all-important step had been taken. The history of this first step is embodied in myths of the New World, no less than of the Old. Tubal-Cain, Dædalus, Hephæstus, Vulcan, Vœlund, Galant, and Wayland the Saxon smith-god, are all legendary variations of the first mastery of the use of the metals; and so, too, the New World has Quetzalcoatl, its divine instructor in the same priceless art.

One of the undeniable truths of ancient history is that, long before Greece rose to prominence as the world's intellectual leader, seafaring races that were bold enough to cross the Atlantic colonized the eastern Mediterranean. The difficulty of crossing that ocean was greater in the first centuries before Christ than at any other time till navigation was revived in the fourteenth century. The discovery of a genuine Phoenician or other inscription, or of a hoard of Assyrian griffins or shekels of the merchant princes of Tyre "that knew the sea," among the still-undiscovered treasures of Montezuma's buried empire or the long-deserted ruins of Central America, would not, therefore, surprise me in the slightest. Such a find would hardly be more unexpected than the Punic hoards discovered in Corvo, the westernmost island of the Azores. The runic monuments of Kingiktorsoak and Igalikko provided proof of the fabled charms of a Hesperian region located within the Arctic circle, as well as of the first real glimpses of the American mainland by Norse voyagers of the tenth century, as told in more than one of their old Sagas. However, it would provide a substantial basis for the legend of Atlantis. However, until such proof is provided, the mythology of Atlantis must remain a myth and pre-Columbian America must continue to be given credit for its achievements.

www.ingramcontent.com/pod-product-compliance
Lightning Source LLC
Chambersburg PA
CBHW061407160726
47995CB00001B/494